"Are We There Yet?"

and 99 Other Reasons Not to Have Kids

"Are We There Yet?"

and 99 Other Reasons Not to Have Kids

Barbara Govednik • Illustrations by Ellen Toomey

Chronicle Books • San Francisco

Book design and illustration: Ellen Toomey

Library of Congress Cataloging-in-Publication Data:
Govednik, Barbara, 1964-
    "Are we there yet?" and 99 other reasons not to have kids / Barbara Govednik.
    p. cm.
ISBN 0-8118-0517-4
    1. Parenting—Humor. 2. Parenthood—Humor. I. Title.
PN6231.P2G68 1995
818'.5402—dc20   94-8833 CIP

Printed in the United States of America.

10 9 8 7 6 5 4 3 2 1

Chronicle Books
275 Fifth Street   Distributed in Canada by Raincoast Books,
San Francisco, CA 94103   8680 Cambie Street, Vancouver, B.C. V6P 6M9

Acknowledgments

Many thanks to my family and friends who helped me (sometimes inadvertently) write this book. Some of you may get an odd sense of déjà vu flipping through these pages, especially Jan Willett, Shannon O'Regan, and Kristen Gallup.

Thank you to my "research assistants" Zach Willet, Nathan Willet, Dara O'Regan, Lauren Gallup, Adam Gallup, Nathan Punwar, Alissa Punwar, Bill Francis, Molly Francis, and Colleen Francis.

Finally, my thanks to Tom for not getting mad when I repeatedly threatened to throw his computer out the window.

1. Your in-laws will visit more often.

2. Your parents will visit
when your in-laws aren't there.

3. Your parents and your in-laws will
become friends and visit together.

4. Car pools.

5. Bake sales.

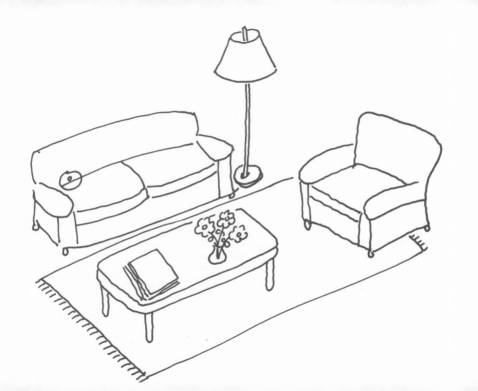

6. A clean house has a fifteen minute half-life.

7. Unlike your oven, kids are not self-cleaning.

8. You'll forget what it's like
   to be out after dark.

9. Catching fifteen minutes of a
   "Roseanne" rerun will be the
   cultural peak of your week.

10. Birthday parties at Chuck E. Cheese's.

11. Kids eat things like hot dogs with butter.

12. You'll judge restaurants
by their kid's menu.

13. You'll be tempted to shop at Baby Gap, where a very small sweater costs as much as the adult version.

14. Shopping at warehouse-sized "baby-rama" stores.

15. Your expensive video camera will catalog many priceless images of your kid waving.

16. Little girls only play dress-up with Mommy's $300 Italian pumps.

17. The most often played tape
in your car will be Raffi
instead of the Rolling Stones.

18. There's a good chance
your kid will actually like rap music.

19. Kids will beat you at Nintendo
every time.

20. You gotta let them win
Chutes and Ladders once in a while.

21. Strollers are part of the grocery cart family and therefore constantly have one wheel that simply refuses to follow the others.

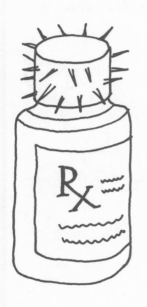

22. Child-proof caps.

23. Plastic cups, plastic bowls, plastic spoons, plastic plates, plastic . . .

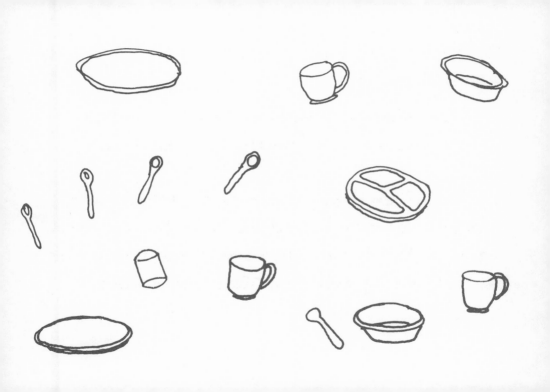

24. Kids remember that you promised them ice cream three years ago.

25. After taking out a second mortgage to pay for a fun-filled week at Disney World, your kid's favorite memory of the trip will be vomiting after Mr. Toad's Wild Ride.

26. Lots of people will let you borrow theirs.

27. Kids will watch the same video
over and over and over and over
and over and over . . .

NAME

COMIC

28. Camps still make parents sew name tags onto everything.

29. Making Halloween costumes.

30. There are no boarding schools
for kindergarten.

31. Once they start school and get more and
more independent, you'll be tempted
to start all over again.

32. Strangers will tell you horror stories about being in labor.

33. Eventually, you will tell strangers horror stories of being in labor.

34. Kids have no use for Kleenex.

35. Spending three hours in the
emergency room while the doctors
remove the penny lodged
in your kid's nose.

36. The tooth fairy now pays at least a buck a tooth.

37. "Calvin and Hobbes" <u>might</u> be based on a true story.

38. Saturday morning cartoons aren't what they used to be.

39. Learning that the words
"mom" and "dad"
refer to you, not your parents.

40. Picking a name that eleven other
children won't have in first grade.

41. No owners manual, no warranty card, no 800-number for faster service.

42. No matter how well you raise them, your kids are still going to blame you.

43. Even if you start today, your kid will be forty-seven years old before you can read every book on child rearing.

44. It never occurs to a kid to go to the bathroom <u>before</u> you bundle them into a snowsuit and boots.

45. Snowsuits have a life of their own.

46. Eventually, they'll insist on dressing themselves.

47. There will be days when the only adult conversation you will have will be with the grocery clerk.

48. You'll ask questions in baby talk, and usually in public.

49. Having a kid's table at Thanksgiving is a sure sign of aging.

50. Admonishing guests at your cocktail party to "use two hands."

51. Everything in your house
will become sticky for no known reason.

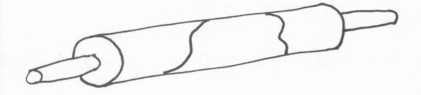

52. Silly Putty on your rolling pin.

53. Dressing to match whatever your toddler is having for lunch since you'll end up wearing half of it.

54. Discovering that "stain-proof carpeting" isn't.

55. Kissing your white sofa goodbye.

56. When kids say, "I have to go to the bathroom," they mean, "I have to go to the bathroom <u>now</u>."

57. Diaper services only pick up once a week.

58. Your childless friends will give them presents like drum sets and xylophones.

59. Kids are ready to leave after the third inning.

60. It's no longer enough to take your kids to every new kids' movie. They'll want the book and the video cassette and the action figures and the plush toys and the drinking glasses and the bed sheets and the breakfast cereal . . .

61. Toys "Я" Us at Christmas time.

62. "Some assembly required."

63. "Batteries not included."

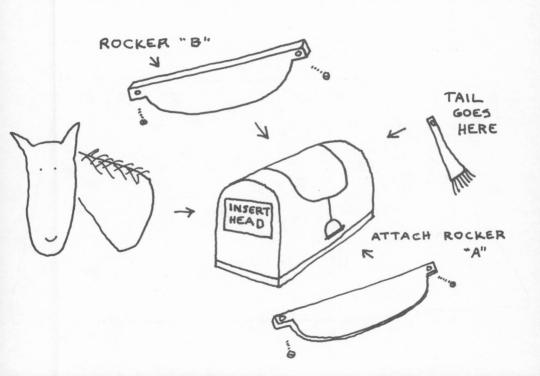

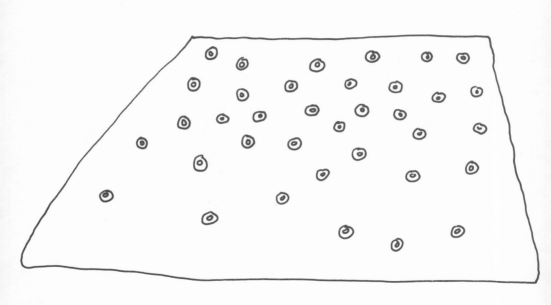

64. Car mats covered with Cheerios.

65. Stepping on Legos.

66. Play-Doh still smells the same.

67. McDonald's Happy Meals
will become haute cuisine.

68. All the pasta in your house will be
shaped like cartoon characters.

69. You won't be able to find
a bandage in your house that's
not decorated with the Peanuts Gang.

MACARONI
& MASHED
BANANA
DINNER

70. Baby food smells
worse than cat food.

71. Maternity leave policies designed for Donna Reed.

72. Giving up your claim to being a "DINK."

73. There's no room in a Miata for you, your spouse, and a baby seat.

74. Airlines do not consider kids carry-on luggage.

75. You <u>will</u> use the television as a baby-sitter.

76. Teenage baby-sitters cancel when they get a better offer.

77. Any offer is better to a teenage baby-sitter.

78. One day, your spouse will look at you and say, "Honey, let's get a minivan."

79. At some point, you will say, "your face is going to freeze like that."

80. Coming up with good reasons why they have to wear a hat but you don't.

81. Not swearing when another driver cuts you off.

82. Not walking when it says, "Don't Walk."

83. Kid's can't talk until they are at least two years old.

84. Once they start talking, just <u>try</u> to get them to stop.

85. "All my friends are wearing them."

86. "Where do babies come from?"

87. "Are we there yet?"

88. Your kid will be allergic to your cat.

89. kids always
want dogs.

90. Remembering to lock the bedroom door.

91. Kids crawl faster than most Olympians can sprint.

92. Sleep.

93. Sex.

94. Breast pumps.

95. Pink and blue.

96. The boys your
    daughter will
    bring home.

97. The girls
    your son won't
    bring home.

98. You didn't start saving for their college education ten years ago.

99. People will think you're having another when actually you're only trying to lose the weight from the first.

100. People will constantly ask you, "When are you going to have another?"